The Good, Bad, and the Ugliest

THE UGLIEST MONSTER OF ALL!!!

CANCER

The Good
The Bad
and
The UGLIEST!!!

THE UGLIEST MONSTER...

CAUSING

ALL

NATIONS

CASUALTIES

EVERY

RACE

CANCER

WE FIGHT TOGETHER!!!

BY:

DEMETRICK MAYS SR

TABLE OF CONTENTS

Chapter One

The

GOOD!!!!!

Not a lot but there is some GOOD!!!

(PREVENT & SURVIVE)

What is Cancer????

Cancer is an undeniable illness, that can start at any point in the Human Body and spread like wildfire, till it consumes it host or is STOPPED and dealt with accordingly!!

Some studies say "Cancer is the splitting of cells that don't stop spreading and ends up spreading into the surrounding tissue and they become abnormal.

The Abnormal Cells and Dying cells are introduced to the new cells and this causes the form of Tumors!!!

Some studies say "Cancer starts when Cells get out of control and

crowd out the normal functioning cells!!
Dr. Sebi says" That ALL Cancer is a form of unattended BAD MUCUS that attacks the body and cells!!!!

Cancer is really a mystery to many, we do more studies and more trials to come up with a cure for some, and yet others, are so rare, there is no cure YET!!!
And I say YET, because we have the will and spirit to SURVIVE!!!
Money and education together are making a big leap with understanding this Monster.
But we all need to do our part because this Monster does not care about us, your Age, Race, Religion

or Gender, it comes hard and most of the times, fast and undetected. It is up to ALL of us, to overcome this Monster together as one, and this might be the way to bring the world CLOSER TOGETHER AS ONE!!!!!

Do you know what Cancer is and How it can Start??

Did you know there is over 200 types of this Monster???

Do you know there are stages as well as groups and classes???

Do you know as an African, what Cancers we need to look out for the most??

Do you know as a Caucasian, what Cancers affects you the Most???

Did you know there are things we can do NOW, so it is hard for this Monster to find you???

Do you know that once this Monster finds you, you still have a chance to escape it???

What Causes Cancer?

Understanding the possible causes of cancer comes down to understanding the causes of the gene and DNA mutations. Chemicals (like carcinogens), radiation, obesity, hormones, chronic inflammation, smoking, viruses, and several other factors have been found to be cancer causing. Some foods are worse for you than others and are increasing your risk of many conditions and diseases. With cancer being one of the worst diseases ever, even with **regularly eating, the cancer-causing foods in our top ten list can also lead to**

heart disease, diabetes, chronic inflammation, and so much more.

The Good thing about this is, we now have a chance to stay on top of screening for our children, and hopefully this will get them in the pattern to visit the doctor on a regular basis. DO NOT, just get the screening, but make sure you, ask your child's doctor questions on any pains or bad bruises, because cancer is a cruel Mystery, that can start from a cut or sore. Sometimes, even a tiny cut can have serious and unexpected consequences. Today's research reveals that even a minor flesh wound can cause previously dormant cancer cells to develop into **tumors.**

Starting our children off eating early in life, will benefit them in so many ways life, but also a comfort in knowing you're doing your best to keep this dangerous Monster at bay!!!

Our children are the future and teaching them the correct way to live and eat and take care of their bodies, will help preserve this world.

Let's pray, that along with everyone doing their part, and with research getting even better. HOPEFULLY, that one day, we can not only CURE this Monster but PREVENT it from showing its ugly face!!!

<u>Good Links and Books to read and Have!!!!!</u> **Sites to visit...**

Blog for a Cure

Cancerwise

The CTCA Blog

Cure Today

Cancer Support Community

Books to read.

The Patient's Playbook by Leslie Michelson

The Emperor of All Maladies: A Biography of Cancer by Siddhartha Mukherjee

The Ugliest Monster of all: Cancer. By Demetrick Mays

Chicken Soup for the Cancer Survivor's Soul

Cancer: What I Wish I Had Known When I Was First Diagnosed: Tips and Advice from a Survivor by Michele Ryan.

Just a couple, (and some great ones to start with at that) BUT WE ARE NOT FINISHED!!! I pray, this will get ALL of us up and get motivated. To not just only getting your families' health on track, but to help and share info with others!!

If cancer is attacking out cells, let's fight back!!!

Pick at least five food that help your cells fight and keep cancer away!!!!!!

•Berries. ...Pomegranates

•Broccoli. ...

•Ginger root. ...

•Nuts and seeds. ...

•Mushrooms. ...

•Fatty fish and seafood. •Avocados. Avocados are high in healthy fats. ...

•Walnuts. Walnuts have many characteristics that make them an excellent food for healthy skin. ...

- Sunflower Seeds. ...
- Sweet Potatoes. ...
- Red or Yellow Bell Peppers. ...
- Tomatoes.
- Seafood. Seafood is an excellent source of protein because it's usually low in fat.
- White-Meat Poultry. ...
- Milk, Cheese, and Yogurt. ...
- Eggs. ...
- Beans. ...
- Pork Tenderloin. ...
- Almonds, Mango, Spinach
- Raisins: 3.1g Protein (6% DV) ...
- Guava: 2.6g Protein (5% DV) ...

- Dates: 2.4g Protein (5% DV) ...
- Olive Oil. ...
- Beets. ...
- Pistachios. ...
- Pomegranate Prunes: 2.2g Protein (4% DV)

Ground flax seed

Garlic

Ginger

Green tea

Turmeric

Vitamin D

Vitamin E

include beta carotene, selenium, and vitamins C and E. Antioxidants reduce the risk of damage from oxidants. Oxidants are substances that can lead to cell damage. Other vitamins and minerals. These include calcium, vitamin D, and B vitamins.

Too much selenium can be toxic, but doses as high as 300 micrograms (mcg) have been shown to reduce certain kinds of cancer, including cancers of the:

esophagus

colon

lung

liver

LET' S DO IT TOGETHER!!!!

Now Black Folk's!!!

When I say, "Let's talk about the bad things that comes when dealing with Cancer", *I'm not talking about the ones born in the month of July*!!

The Bad things about this Monster is no laughing matter at all, and the worst part about it is, it does not stop growing and Attacking us, even at a very early age!!

Cancer is a BAD Monster!!!!!

Cancer is responsible for more than 15% of the world deaths!!!

Cancer seems to attack the poverty-stricken cultures more!!!

Cancer LOVES sugar!!

Cancer is a very Fast runner!!

Cancer is a life changer!!

Cancer will make one prioritize things in your life!!!

Cancer is 5-10% a genetic link!!!

Cancer comes from Sleep deprivation!!! (Colin).

Cancer can come from type 1 diabetes, and asthma (Children at risk).

Cancer comes from Obesity!!!

Cancer effects Non-melanoma skin human more!!!

Blacks on GRILLING and how-to Avoiding exposure to Cancer!!!! (We know we

love us some BBQ But, we MUST Love Life even MORE!!)

They say there are two cancer-causing (carcinogenic) byproducts associated with barbecuing red meat, poultry, lamb, pork, and fish. The first is a carcinogen called heterocyclic amines (HCAs). HCAs are formed due to the high temperatures occurring when meat is overcooked or char-grilled. It is proven that when HCAs were fed in the diet, Animals developed cancers in many organs, including the colon, breast, and prostate. The second carcinogen associated with barbecuing is polycyclic aromatic hydrocarbons (PAHs). They are formed when fat drips onto the coal or hot surface. The smoke carries the PAHs to the food. They can also form directly on the food when it is charred or over-cooked.

How to prepare food, so they are HEALTIER!!!!

•Don't get too hot: The USDA Recommended Safe Minimum Internal Temperatures are:

◦Steaks & roasts - 145°F

◦Fish - 145°F

◦Pork - 160°F

◦Ground beef - 160°F

◦Chicken breasts - 165°F

◦Whole poultry - 165°F

•Trim the fat: **Go for leaner cuts of meat!!**

•Take time to marinate:

•Keep it clean: Keep the oil and grease off your grill by turning up the heat to high and closing the lid for about 10 minutes

Standing near the grill for long periods of time may also increase your risk of health hazards

•Avoiding direct exposure of meat to an open flame or a hot metal surface and avoiding prolonged cooking times.

•Using a microwave oven to cook meat prior to exposure to high temperatures.

•Continuously flip and turn your meat over while grilling.

• refraining from using gravy made from meat.

Great sites with detailed info, https://www.mdanderson.org/publications/focused-on-health/july-2014/barbecue-cancer.html

Chapter Two:

The Bad

DISRESPECTFUL MONSTER!!!!!

(VICTIMS)

Death comes in many ways and we never know the hour or day it will fall upon us!!!!

Unfortunately, I have witness death in different stages to where, I know that we can make it HARDER on ourselves, a little more COMFORTABLE for ourselves, and even help put a STOP to it!!!

Most say it is your attitude towards it, some say it is the medicine you take, some say it is your support group you have around you, we now know it is what you put in your body and how you treat your body...

So, if we take the good out of all these things then maybe we can stand a chance against this Monster!!!!!!

One of the worst ways I have seen someone suffer is AIDS and CANCER!!!!

And there are so many differ forms of Cancer to it is now taking over the death toll race!!!!!

WHAT CAN YOU DO TO HELP PREVENT OR STOP CANCER????

Living our best life is what we all want to do, but if it is gone to cost you in the long run, why not take a couple precautions now to help yourself in the future???

Life has its own curve balls and rollercoasters of its own to throw at us, and to be stricken with this Monster will make one feel HELPLESS!!!!

Learning to balance our lives now, maybe we can help the next generation move forward with out so many deaths from this Monster!!!

The one true thing that I have learned in this lifetime is, the better you prepare yourself for something, the better chance you have at succeeding at it or overcoming it!!!

WHY NOT PREPARE OURSEVLES FOR THIS MONSTER??? BECAUSE IT SEEMS LIKE IT IS PREPARED FOR US!!

Getting prepared and staying on course, will take A LOT of will power, See, I rather put forth the will power instead of the Have to power. And that means:

DON'T WAIT UNTILL WE HAVE NO CHOICE BUT TO BE STRONG!!

Choices about your health, will have to be made, sooner or later, we know now it is best to take the option now, instead of them forced on you later!!!

Having a plan for our Children, is the main reason for this book/guideline, and maybe we can start a road map of success against this Monster!!!

LET's TAKE ACTION NOW!!!!!!!!!!

Find ways to get involved and educate yourself!!!!!!!!

Find out about your family's health issues and stay on top of them!!!!

Find a great diet now and exercise schedule that you can stick to!!!

Find great organizations that will help when needed!!!

Find out who is your support team!!!!!

Find out what works for you, to stay in a good place, even when it is storming in your life!!!!!!!

With each stage of Cancer, it is growing and getting stronger, so we must be aggressive in the way we attack this Monster!!!!

With all that we must endure when dealing with this Monster from, Emotion to finances and losing Love one, we see this Monster is UNBEARING, UNCARING and very DISRESPECTFUL!!!

One must surround themselves with an AWESOME Support team during these times, this Monster will attack your:

Belief and religion, Your Families Love for you, Your Friends Love for you, Your Finances, Your Love for life, and more!!

We tend to Question God on all bad things that happens to us, and this will put you in a place of not just where you will question GOD, but also finding yourself either cursing GOD or straying away from the word!!

I have heard testimony of others that have dealt with differ emotions and scares when dealing with this, and I know, from first-hand experience, that you will get to a point of not knowing what to do and what prayers to say that will work???

How can you let this happen to my son your child or do you care?? Is what I would question GOD on a lot when my boy got sick!! My son was giving two to three months to live, and my prayer and conversation with GOD then was “LORD HOW”?? “LORD WHY”?? and “LORD WHY ME”

Lord what have I done to deserve this?? Lord I do my best to live right and obey you and this is how you repay me??? So many mixed emotions going on in your mind but also at the same time I’m praying for better!!

My Fathers cancer was diagnosed when he was in stage 4, Lung cancer and was given a couple months to live, no matter what the prayer was that we said, he was gone in a couple months...

My son’s cancer was diagnosed in stage 4, Kidney cancer, and he was given two to three months to live. The prayers then seem to work at times and not work at others and he lived for two more years, where in the end was called home!!

For those two years of running back and forth to the hospital, and with his insurance, not covering everything, I was broke, hurting, and very frustrated financially!!! Had to take FMLA at work, so I can be with my son when sick but keep my job!!!

I was not working much, and my savings account was starting to be depleted, this will leave you guessing, if GOD is on your side?????

GOD WHY ME!!!!

WHAT DID I DO TO DESERVE THIS??

DON'T YOU LOVE ME??

DO YOU HATE ME???

WHAT DID I DO WRONG??

Such an emotional rollercoaster that you're on, that you're not sure what to feel beside the pain that is going on inside is real!!!

You start to turn to earthly things to help calm yourself like drinking or drugs, because you feel that GOD is not doing nothing to stop the pain!!!

My Dealings with the Monster!!!

Sickle Cell Trait can turn into Cancer!!

I have had many Family members that have had close encounters with this Monster, some survive and some fall victim of its raft!! From a young age I have had dealings with Monsters of death, but the worsts have been Aid's and Cancer. Both bad boys but both preventable!!!

My first remembrance of this Monster was with my Father, MY HERO!!

The strongest man that I ever known and the person that taught me to walk like a man!!! I Saw my Father go through a lot of things but this Monster here, was, Silent, Quick and deadly!!!!

My dad had been through a couple car accidents, even an explosion, where he was burned majority of his body and was in the hospital for months, but nothing even close to this bully called cancer!!!!!!

Found out he had it at stage 4, and the time he was diagnosed with Lung Cancer, he was single and living alone!! My Step Mother, which he was married to for over 20 years, stepped in and became his caretaker.

An illness can bring love together or tear it apart, depending on the hearts, and the situation during these times.

Working his whole life doing drywall and building homes, plus a smoker, we were not sure if it was from the asbestos work or smoking. But one thing for sure he had it and had to put up a fight now to stop it!!!!

One of the worse things about finding out about this Monster is, when it is to late!!!

Stage 1 and 2 will give you a better chance, but still a hard pill to swallow, so let's stay on top of our health, so we can survive and live a better life style thereafter.

Finding out about the Monster when in stage 3 or 4, is the hardest pill to swallow, and to try and get control of!!!!!

Finding out that my dad had cancer was a big blow to the family, we all had to pull together and do what was needed for him to be comfortable and Happy.

Hospice stepped in and helped a lot also, but it is nothing you can do when one wants to do for themselves and can't anymore and have to rely on others!!! My father did great until he needed assistance to the bathroom, and that is when he gave up !!! The type of strength my dad showed his whole life, wouldn't let his pride go that far.

I think within four months of finding out about this Monster, my father was called home...

After my Father passed, I really did not see this monster up close for a while, but it was still around, because, I kept hearing stories and seeing other losing love ones!!!

My Father passed in 2006, I had to learn to live without him from that point and now, we come to 2016 and find out my son has Cancer!!!!

My son was healthy his whole life, up until age 18, and even then, when we took him to the hospital and doctor, they were unable to find this Monster, because they were not aware of this Type Cancer, and overlooked it a couple times...

This is another reason for this ligature to update us all, on small things luring before that become a problem!!!

Age 18, my son was trying to get his life on track, my boy started working two jobs, while getting his G.E.D. Riding his bike, back and forth to school and work, I would help him out also, because I was proud, he was doing good.

He started having chest and back pains around the beginning of the year 2015, within three months, he had been to the two different ER Rooms and his primary doctor, but all they said was, he was still growing, and the pain was cartilage still growing and due to sports and exercise....

Once they found out what was causing the problem in my son, they told us is was Cancer, in stage 4 and there was pretty much nothing they could do!!! They gave my boy two to three months to live and they had no plan for treatment!!!!

This was a very devastating blow to us, when we put our trust in them to find out the problem before It is to late!!! But they knew nothing of this Monster and where it hides its face, so getting mad at them, was not the thing to do!!!!

Praying and figuring out a way to attack this monster, was the only thing we had to do!! Networking with other doctors, around the world, and come up with a Game plan for my son and others!

I ended up giving up just about everything, from my own place to my pets.

I ended up moving in with my sister, and had to give up my two dogs, my girl dog Char and my boy Casper!!

Very hard decisions to make, but my son's health took priority over everything!!

Had to go on FMLA at work (I can miss family sick days, but no pay), I was living at the hospital more than I was at my own house, it was getting very expensive!!!

They said, "Two to Three months to live"?? My God Blessed my son with Two more years of Life, Plus, a Beautiful Child, before he passed!!!

Just to prove that Cancer, does not care about who are what you are, even our dog Char, has cancer and only a couple weeks to live!!!!! My dog will not eat or even move much, the only thing that can help, is if she gets some steroids, and that's only for a little comfort and to help her eat.

It seems it is all about money to stretch life to its fullest or should we let go and let god in cases like this?

So, a year after burring my son I now left with the choice to go see my dog get buried or just remember the good times we shared!!!!

Buck Cancer and I mean that in the best bad way possible!

We need to buck it the way, it is fucking up our lives!!!

Everyone is excused to say this just one time: no matter what just let it out one good time!!!!

"BUCK CANCER"!!!!!!

Can we ALL stop and take a moment of silence for the lives taken by cancer??

Signs that the UGLY Monster might be lurking around your closet!!!!!

- Persistent cough or blood-tinged saliva
- A change in bowel habits
- Blood in the stool
- Unexplained anemia (low blood count)
- Breast lump or breast discharge
- Lumps in the testicles
- A change in urination
- Hoarseness
- Persistent lumps or swollen glands
- Obvious change in a wart or a mole
- Indigestion or difficulty swallowing
- Feeling Bloated
- Skin Irregularities
- Unexpected Weight Loss
- Burning Hearts
- Feeling Feverish

SORRY TO SAY IT GET's UGLIER!!!!!!!!

Next steps to take once you have these are critical!!!

Chapter 3
The
UGLIEST!!!

The ugliest things we must face!!!!

(The AFTERMATH)

They are gone home to be with the LORD now!!!! They put up a good fight and no matter what events took place, no matter how much praying was done, and support and Love shown.

They are in a better place Now, while we are here to grieve and try and get Life back on track, the best we can, without that Love one around anymore!

For me, getting back to life without my son, was like trying to live without part of my heart!! How does one do that??

That meant trying to get back to an even breaking point with my finances and trying to rebuild my savings account!!

That meant being as strong as I can, for whenever I run into a person that might bring it back up!!

That means, making the Holiday, at least a good day, because they don't feel like Holidays anymore!!!!

That means, I must live life more cautiously of things, that can cause me the face the same faith!!!

That means, I need to do better, so I don't end up losing to the same monster, I been trying to defeat for years!!!

In my case, for two years I was not able to work a full 40 hours better yet 25 some weeks!! Having full custody of my son and a single parent, I had a friend at the time, but I was the primary bread winner and the bills did not care about my son having cancer, not even the Landlord or any other bill collector... my pay coming in was not enough money, going out to take care everything.

So, I moved in with my sister and had to roommate with her for a while and cut back on a lot my personal fun and spending!!

The ugliest part is, having to move on without the loves that I have lost, but, yet still, I still must deal with the monster that is here affecting my dog, and now we found out, my younger brother has prostate cancer!!!

So many families must go through rebuilding their lives after taking care of a love one for a while then losing them to Cancer and then it might not stop there!!!

So, if there is one thing you can take from this book is:

Get LIFE INSURANCE!!!

Get regular cancer screenings on you and the Children and Pet's if you chose!!

Take at least 5 cooking tips to try and start eating better!!

Understand what is to come and try to prepare for it. Medical savings account, support team in place, Prayer partners,

TIMES WILL GET HARD!!!!

THERE WILL BE TIMES YOU WANT TO GIVE UP!!!!!

THERE ARE TIMES YOU NEED COMFORT FROM OTHERS!!!!

TIMES WHEN YOU WANT TO BE ALONE!!!!!

Here are some Prayers and tips on how I got through a lot of rough days and nights and some tips from others also!!!!!!

PRAYERS:

For Strength.

Deuteronomy 31:6 - Be strong and of a good courage, fear not, nor be afraid of them: for the LORD thy God, he [it is] that doth go with thee; he will not fail thee, nor forsake thee.

Philippians 4:13 - I can do all things through Christ which strengtheneth me.

Psalms 31:24 - Be of good courage, and he shall strengthen your heart, all ye that hope in the LORD.

1 Corinthians 16:13 - Watch ye, stand fast in the faith, quit you like men, be strong.

Just a couple but pls find ones that works for you???

For healing:

Jeremiah 33:6 - Behold, I will bring it health and cure, and I will cure them, and will reveal unto them the abundance of peace and truth.

James 5:15 - And the prayer of faith shall save the sick, and the Lord shall raise him up; and if he have committed sins, they shall be forgiven him.

James 5:14 - Is any sick among you? let him call for the elders of the church; and let them pray over him, anointing him with oil in the name of the Lord:

Psalms 41:3 - The LORD will strengthen him upon the bed of languishing: thou wilt make all his bed in his sickness.

For Understanding of Death:

Revelation 21:4 - And God shall wipe away all tears from their eyes; and there shall be no more death, neither sorrow, nor crying, neither shall there be any more pain: for the former things are passed away.

Ecclesiastes 12:7 - Then shall the dust return to the earth as it was: and the spirit shall return unto God who gave it.

Matthew 10:28 - And fear not them which kill the body but are not able to kill the soul: but rather fear him which is able to destroy both soul and body in hell.

Romans 6:23 - For the wages of sin [is] death; but the gift of God [is] eternal life through Jesus Christ our Lord.

Prayer are all we have sometimes, so please find some good ones and surround yourself with pray partners!!

For Hope:

Romans 12:12 - Rejoicing in hope; patient in tribulation; continuing instant in prayer;

Mark 9:23 - Jesus said unto him, If thou canst believe, all things [are] possible to him that believeth.

Jeremiah 17:7 - Blessed [is] the man that trusteth in the LORD, and whose hope the LORD is.

Tips for those hard days and Nights.

I healed by writing a book when my son passed of cancer, “GOD HAS SPOKEN” hoping to help and educate other, helped me.

Reaching out to close love ones that I knew could lift me up and are able to comfort me.

I even made a play list of songs, so I can cry and get it out of the way and get my day started, you’re going to have those days so be ready and prepared!!

Summary of what we need to do???

With over 200+ cancer out here, we need to know the ones that are more acceptable to you and your family!!!

That the necessary steps to prepare your life better to avoid this Monster!!!!

Find a healthier way to prepare foods for you and your family!!!!!!

Read up on ways to protect your cells!!

Keep enjoying life just in a better way for a longer time.....

If you don't do this for you, do it for your children and the next generations that will walk the land!!!

Checklist:

What type of Cancers will affect me?? __

What Cancer are hereditary to me??___

What illnesses are there in my Family___??

What foods can I start eating now to help me be healthier??____

What foods do I need to Quit eating??___

Do I exercise enough or too much??_____

Are my cells healthy??_____

About the Author:

Demetrick Lenard Mays Sr.

Born 11/23/1974 to Gwendolyn E. Jenkins that passed at the age 42 of AIDS and David L Mays that passed at the age 64 of lung cancer.

I was married for 14 years, where I took care of four beautiful children along with my son Lil Dee. After the marriage was over it was just my son and me. I was a single parent, Black man trying to make things better for my son and I. Always in church with my boy and always trying to lead by example. No record and not being a deadbeat were the main things I wanted my boy to learn. I was a

Handworker and tried to be the best Father I could be. At age 18 my son was diagnosed with Kidney cancer (RMC). After several trips to the ER for chest and backpains, they finally found cancer growing inside my boy and told us it was in stage 4 and he only had two months to live. He lived for two years and had a baby girl also. After putting up a great fight with this monster my son was called home in 2017 at age 20. My dog just past of cancer and my little brother has prostate cancer!!!

THIS MONSTER WILL NEVER GIVE UP!!!!! SO, I WILL NEVER GIVE UP!!! WHEN WE MEET AGAIN, I WILL BE BETTER PREPARED FOR THIS MONSTER!!!

I am writing this book to reach out and help others understand the importance in living a better healthier life!! We must start somewhere, and everyone is not going to tell you the truth about things, so do your research and find what mindset you need to have to avoid this monster and how to put up a great fight if you do encounter this monster!!

Another book from Author: God has Spoken

GOD HAS SPOKEN!!

We put no trust in mans word,,

-We Wait-

"Until God has Spoken"

BY: Demetrick L. Mays S.R.

Made in the USA
Middletown, DE
26 December 2021

57038538R00040